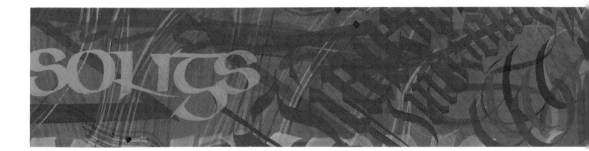

WIND SONGS

Timothy R. Botts

TYNDALE

HOUSE

PUBLISHERS

INC.

WHEATON

ILLINOIS

A special thanks to:

Takao and Momoko Ohmori
for the Japanese papers

Chuck Peterson
for his handmade marbled paper

Gil Beers
for the monarch butterfly

Jim Stambaugh
for his tough words of advice

Deb Copelin
for securing permission of lyrics

Vicki deVries
for polishing my words

W I N D S O N G S

Library of Congress Catalog Card Number
89-50698
ISBN 0-8423-8252-6
Copyright ©1989 by Timothy R. Botts
All rights reserved
Printed in the United States of America

2   3   4   5   6   7   93   92   91   90   89

To my grandfather

BARTON BRADLEY BOTTS

who by way of eighty-eight keys

taught me how to feel

INTRODUCTION

My mother sang hymns while washing dishes. ◆ My father sang in the church choir. My grandfather played the church organ and taught me piano for seven years. ◆ And my great aunt was the choral director at the local high school. ◆ Music was in my veins, too. I sang in the church choir, then in school choirs, and later accompanied my high-school choir on the piano. ◆ A wonderful art teacher in grade school thought I had artistic ability and encouraged my talent. In order to affirm my work, my parents encouraged me by buying special frames for my pictures and hanging them up around the house. I began seeing myself as an artist. ◆ Later, as a high-school student, I came to an occupational fork in the road and made the conscious decision to be a visual artist. At the university I was exposed to calligraphy, which is also called "the dance of the pen." Its lyrical quality brought music and art together for me. ◆ After doing the book Doorposts, which was based on the Bible, I found it hard to imagine using any lesser text for another book. However, I came to realize that most of the great music of the Christian faith has come as a result of deep spiritual experiences. The hymn writers' words are my testimony as well. ◆ And so I have set them to music—the music of my pen—for you.

Both Jews and Christians share a common heritage, one that I deeply appreciate. After all, God chose the Hebrew race to introduce himself to mankind. And they have faithfully preserved the Torah through millennia.

Several years ago I had the opportunity to attend a bar mitzvah. To my delight, I discovered this hymn by Isaac Watts in the back of their book of service—another common link.

I created the circular background movement with a shaving brush.

NEXT SPREAD:
In compiling these hymns, I was impressed by how many lyrics have essentially the same message, in spite of sectarian lines and changing times. This medley is one of several throughout this book.

The Latin text Sanctus comes directly from the Scripture, making these the oldest words in this book. The more recent English is superimposed to give a sense of history. Reginald Heber, Anglican bishop to Calcutta early in the nineteenth century, wrote the second hymn below.

O
GOD
OUR HELP
IN AGES PAST
OUR HOPE FOR YEARS
TO COME
OUR SHELTER FROM
THE STORMY BLAST
AND OUR ETERNAL HOME
BEFORE THE HILLS IN ORDER STOOD
OR EARTH RECEIVED HER FRAME
FROM EVERLASTING THOU ART GOD
TO ENDLESS YEARS THE SAME

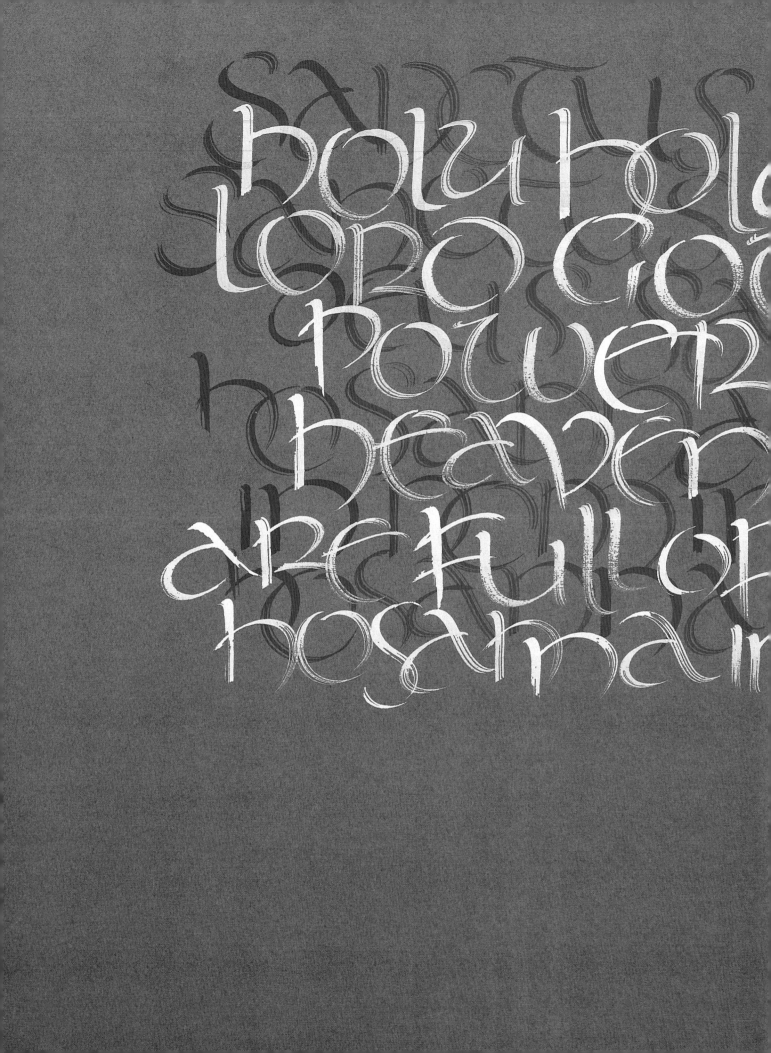

SANCTUS
SANCTUS
HOLY
OF
AND MIGHT
AND EARTH
YOUR GLORY
THE HIGHEST

HOLY · HOLY · HOLY
THOUGH THE DARKNESS HIDE THEE
THOUGH THE EYE OF SINFUL MAN
THY GLORY MAY NOT SEE
ONLY THOU ART HOLY
THERE IS NONE BESIDE THEE
PERFECT IN POWER · IN LOVE AND PURITY

Praise God from

Frail children of dust, and feeble as frail

Praise Him, all

IN THEE DO WE TRUST· NOR FIND THEE

Praise Him above,

Thy mercies how tender, **HOW FIRM TO THE END**

Praise Father,

OUR MAKER, Defender, Redeemer &

ATOM

BUTTERFLY

COMET

DOLPHIN

EVERGREEN

FLAMINGO

GIRAFFE

HUNGARIAN

ICICLE

JADE

KANGAROO

LOBSTER

MOUNTAIN

NIGHTINGALE

OCEAN

PEACOCK

QUARK

RASPBERRY

SNOWFLAKE

TIGER

URANIUM

VIOLET

WATERMELON

XYLEM

YEMENITE

ZEBRA

whom all blessings flow

creatures here below

TO FAIL

ye heavenly host

Son and Holy Ghost

friend

PREVIOUS SPREAD:
This medley features what has come to be known as the Doxology, or hymn of praise to God. It was written by Thomas Ken, chaplain to King Charles II of England, near the middle of the sixteenth century.

The vertical relationship of praise lent itself to the alphabetical litany of created things on the right-hand side.

Interspersed between the lines is the last verse of "O Worship the King" by Robert Grant. The last line contains a list of God's names with amazing contrasts.

THIS SPREAD:
The writings of Irish woman Cecil Alexander (1823-1895) and a traditional spiritual combine to celebrate the God who not only makes but also cares for his creation.

I enjoy the extraordinary variety clustered in the palm of God's hand. Things would not be as wonderful without such creative extravagance. As great as the creation is, the Creator is greater still.

NEXT SPREAD:
When my wife told a friend in our hometown about this book project, she urged me to include this hymn, her church's favorite.

As I read through the words that span the celestial and the commonplace, I agreed. Herbert Brokering's lyrics reflect the poet's wonderful gift to hear the music in our everyday labor and recreation.

Echoing the psalmist's command, I, too, praise the Lord with this new song.

HE'S GOT

HE'S GOT

THE WIND AND THE RAIN IN HIS HANDS
HE'S GOT THE TINY LITTLE BABY IN HIS HANDS
HE'S GOT YOU AND ME·BROTHER··YOU AND ME·SISTER·IN HIS HANDS

ALL THINGS
BRIGHT AND
beautiful
ALL CREATURES
GREAT
AND small
AND ALL THINGS
WISE
AND
wonderful
THE LORD GOD MADE THEM ALL

THE WHOLE WORLD IN HIS HANDS

LOUD, HUMMING CELLOS

clashing cymbals

MARVELOUS THINGS. I TOO WILL PRAISE HIM WITH A NEW SONG

GINES
AND
STEEL

CLASS
ROOMS
AND
LABS

ATHLETE
AND BAND
AND BAND
AND BAND

LOUD
POUNDING
HAMMERS
STONE

Loud
boiling test tubes

Loud cheering people

BUILDING WORKERS

GREAT
is Thy faith
morning by morning
ALL I HAVE NEEDED

fulness O GOD MY FATHER

new mercies I see

THY HAND HATH PROVIDED

GREAT is Thy faithfulness LORD

unto me

Jesu

يسوع

Иисус

JESUS! THE NAME HIGH OVER ALL

ANGELS AND MEN

PREVIOUS SPREAD:
Jim Draper tells the story of meeting the hymn writer Thomas Chisholm at age eighty-five. He was impressed by how much the old man reminded him of Christ. In contrast, Chisholm said of himself, "I'm just an old shoe."

His inspiration for this hymn was the Book of Lamentations, which overwhelmed him with God's faithfulness. When God enables us to see each day as a gift, we, too, will be overwhelmed with this thought.

Like frames on a filmstrip, the row of sunrises portrays the dependability of day and night.

THIS SPREAD:
This is one of Charles Wesley's six-thousand hymns written in the eighteenth century.

The flags all bear the name of Jesus in various languages around the world. His authority flourishes as the One uniquely risen from the dead—separating him from all other great names in history.

Notice the gradually increasing space between the letters below the banners. My intention was to create a ripple effect.

ישוע

JESUS

Jezus

IN HELL OR EARTH OR SKY

BEFORE IT FALL

AND DEVILS FEAR AND FLY

On our first family vacation to the Pacific Northwest in 1987, I witnessed the stately forests of Washington State.

When I began to visualize this anonymous German hymn, my vacation experience immediately came to mind. No cathedral could have equaled that space for worship.

With this slender letter style I tried to capture the perspective of endless trees. A strong sense of the vertical dominated my consciousness.

NEXT SPREAD:

Frederick Lehman's early twentieth-century lyrics convey the inadequacy of words to describe the extent of God's love. Still, it is the response of love to try.

One might also title this a hymn for calligraphers, or scribes as we are sometimes called. True parchment, referred to in the verse, is made from lambskin.

Because of its use through many centuries, some very old documents have survived to the present. Paper would not have lasted as long.

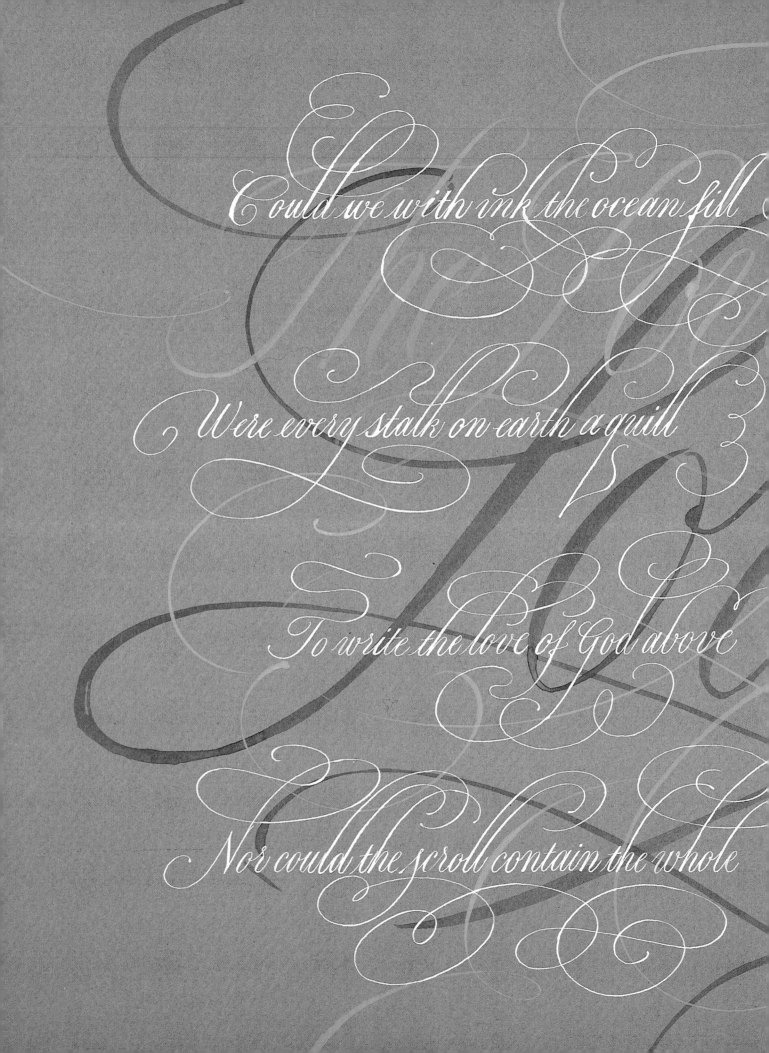

Could we with ink the ocean fill

Were every stalk on earth a quill

To write the love of God above

Nor could the scroll contain the whole

And were the skies of parchment made

And every man a scribe by trade

Would drain the ocean dry

Though stretched from sky to sky

Karl Barth, the great German theologian, was once asked to give the most profound statement of religion. He replied with the words of this simplest of songs.

I decided on this tall, thin format to emphasize each word and to slow down the reader. No flowery words here. Every word counts.

JESUS ♥ me
THIS
I KNOW
for the
Bible
tells
me
·SO·
little
ones
to
HIM
·belong·
They
ARE
weak
BUT
HE
is
STRONG

It seemed natural to choose a polar projection of the earth to symbolize God's entrance into history through his only-begotten Son.

Think of Christmas from God's perspective: one billion Christians joined together each year to celebrate Jesus' birth! I associated Isaac Watts's words with the joy of watching my children play handbells at school.

NEXT SPREAD:
One of my assignments in college was to capture on paper the lights of the Pittsburgh skyline. What an odd sight my buddy and I must have made at night as we sat painting on the hillside by candlelight.

The words and the music of this Appalachian carol are inseparable—so well do they work together to convey the mystery one feels when contemplating the Incarnation. I appreciate the humility of the writer's testimony, which also retains the sense of wonder because everything is not explained.

Joy to the world The Lord is come

Let earth receive her king

Let every heart prepare Him room

And heaven and nature sing

He rules the world with truth and grace

And makes the nations prove

The glories of His righteousness

And wonders of His love

I wonder as I wander

How Jesus the Savior

For poor, ornery people

I wonder as I wander

out under the sky
did come for to die
like you and like I
out under the sky

I danced in the morning when the world was begun
And I danced in the moon and the stars and the sun
And I came down from heaven and I danced on the
At Bethlehem I had my birth
I danced for the scribe and the Pharisee
But they would not dance and they wouldn't follow
I danced for the fishermen, for James and for John
They came with me and the dance went on
I danced on a Friday when the sky turned black
It's hard to dance with the devil on your back
They buried my body and they thought I'd gone
But I am the dance and I still live on

DANCE, THEN, WHEREVER YOU MAY BE
I AM THE LORD OF THE DANCE
I'LL LEAD YOU ALL WHEREVER R
I WILL LEAD YOU ALL

earth

me

SAID HE
YOU MAY BE
IN THE DANCE, SAID HE

PREVIOUS SPREAD:
I like this American Shaker melody because it makes me want to dance. The tune invites me to join in. It inspires such joy! Jesus is like that … arms wide open … inviting us to be part of his kingdom-building.

A unique feature of the lyrics is the use of the first person—Jesus speaking to us. The broad scope of time spans from creation to the present.

I allowed my writing to relax to fit the folk nature of the song. The letters bounce in fairly regular rhythm, taking cues from impending ascenders and descenders.

THIS SPREAD:
The traditional Irish melody "Londonderry Air" gave me the perfect opportunity to use this less familiar Celtic style of writing. Mine is a takeoff from one of the most valuable books in the world, The Book of Kells. This illuminated manuscript of the Gospels has survived twelve centuries and can still be viewed at Trinity College in Dublin.

My knotwork is considerably less sophisticated than the aforementioned work. Nevertheless, it symbolizes the crown of pain that Jesus endured. And as William Fullerton wrote, "He lives to stand beside us in our own pain."

CANNOT TELL

how silently he suffered
as with his peace
he graced this place of tears
or how his heart
upon the cross was broken
the crown of pain
to three and thirty years
but this I know
he heals the brokenhearted
and stays our sin
and calms our lurking fear
and lifts the burden
from the heavy laden
for yet the savior
savior of the world is here

My mother frequently sang this song over the kitchen sink. So my choice to include this one is hardly objective.

Still, it offers something more than sentimentality—the hope in which she rests. George Bernard further developed that hope in the fourth verse: "Then He'll call me someday to my home far away, where His glory forever I'll share."

Carving, I decided, was the only way to capture the ruggedness.

On a hill far away
stood an old rugged cross
The emblem of suffering and shame
And I love that old cross
where the dearest and best
For a world of lost sinners was slain
So I'll cherish the old rugged cross
Til my trophies at last I lay down
I will cling to the old rugged cross
And exchange it someday
for a crown

WHEN I SURVEY THE

ON WHICH THE PRI

WONDROUS CROSS

NCE OF GLORY DIED

My richest gain I count but loss
And pour contempt on all my pride

WERE
THE WHOLE
REALM OF
NATURE MINE

that were a present
far too small

Love so amazing
so divine

DEMANDS
MY SOUL
MY LIFE
MY ALL

PREVIOUS SPREAD:

Isaac Watts, known as the father of English hymns, penned these words in 1707. They have since been called the greatest hymn lyrics in our language.

My father taught me the importance of dynamics. He still gets upset when someone directs music like this without regard for the meaning of the lyrics. His sensitivity to tempo, volume, and grammatical breaks has influenced me to be sensitive as I visually interpret such texts.

THIS SPREAD:

The presence of blood sacrifice in the Bible is evidence to some people that Christianity is uncivilized. Yet such sacrifice is what our holy God requires in order to forgive us for breaking his laws.

Jesus was willing to endure what is repulsive to us. And he did it on our behalf once and for all.

So, what is our celebration based on? The fact that when we accept Christ's sacrifice for us, we are acquitted!

The English poet William Cowper wrote this hymn in 1771 perhaps to remind us of that very fact.

THERE IS A
FOUNTAIN
FILLED
WITH BLOOD
DRAWN FROM
IMMANUEL'S
VEINS

and sinners plunged beneath that flood

lose
all their
guilty stains

This testimony written by Dora Greenwell in the 1800s should appeal to the systematic thinker who honestly examines the Gospel accounts. In contrast to the pride of much educational research, discovering Jesus brings us to our knees.

Recently a friend pointed out that at first glance, much of my work does not appear particularly pleasing. Fortunately, he went on to say that reading the text brings understanding and appreciation. This piece is a case in point.

The just dying for the unjust is simply not a message to decorate.

NEXT SPREAD:
In contrast to the reasoned response of the previous hymn writer, this traditional spiritual spills with emotion. We are gripped by the awful realization that we are participants in Christ's crucifixion. Then our despair turns into hallelujahs for his triumph over death. Words that come as the result of deep experience ring true here.

My goal for this piece was to express in my own medium the same intensity as a black gospel choir in performance.

"Christ

I AM NOT SKILLED TO UNDERSTAND
WHAT GOD HAS WILLED, WHAT GOD HAS PLANNED

I ONLY KNOW AT HIS RIGHT HAND
IS ONE WHO IS MY SAVIOR

I take Him at His word indeed:

died for sinners," this I read

For in my heart I find a need
of Him to be my Savior

That He should leave His place on high
and come for sinful man to die

You count it strange? So once did I
BEFORE I KNEW MY SAVIOR

WHEN HE ROSE UP FROM THE DEAD?
FEEL LIKE SHOUTING GLORY GLORY

Christian Gellert wrote this
German hymn in the 1700s.
Because I grew up with lively
church music, I remember
labeling a tune like this dull and
dead. As a young adult, I began
to realize that the depth of certain
truths calls for equally serious
music.

How different the range of
lyrics that express the same
profound truths of the gospel!

Jesus lives, and so shall I:
Death, thy sting is gone forever!
He for me hath deigned to die,
Lives the bands of death to sever.
He shall raise me from the dust:
Jesus is my hope and trust.

YESTERDAY HE DIED FOR ME-THIS IS HISTORY

J E S U S

Today He lives for me

C H

this is victory

TOMORROW HE COMES FOR ME. THIS IS MYSTERY

IS IT THE LORD

PREVIOUS SPREAD:

Jack Wyrtzen, who wrote this song in the 1960s, divided time into three parts—the way we usually think of it.

Four independent Gospel writers recorded the account of Jesus' death within thirty to fifty years of the event. This prompted me to simulate an early manuscript for this stanza.

The current rage among calligraphers is free-style brush writing. I used that style to celebrate Jesus' present reign in heaven. Imagining the letterforms of the future stretched the limits of my creativity.

THIS SPREAD:

One of the most moving experiences I have ever had with music was seeing a local drama troupe perform Godspell. These thirteenth-century lyrics by St. Richard of Chichester were sung and signed by the players for the actor representing Jesus.

Thinking about how each day of our life is unique, I took the same four letters of this litany and made each one different from the rest. The result—a picture portraying the exciting life of one living in the pursuit of God.

O DEAR LORD

THREE THINGS I PRAY:

TO SEE THEE MORE CLEARLY

LOVE THEE MORE DEARLY

FOLLOW THEE MORE NEARLY

Silently now
I wait for Thee
Ready, my God,
Thy will to see

PREVIOUS SPREAD:

Clara Scott wrote this song in the late 1800s. When we open ourselves up to God's will, I believe he inspires us to be our best. Others more gifted to do skillful work may do so without acknowledging him. Either way God manifests himself and receives praise. Perhaps the difference lies in the joy that worshipers receive.

I used gold throughout this book to represent the Lord's Presence.

THIS SPREAD:

This particular text is J. Edwin Orr's expansion of Psalm 139:23. It reminded me of Moses' encounter with God at the burning bush. No wonder the letters took on a wild, flamelike character.

Yet they are dwarfed by the larger, all-encompassing flames. I found it helpful to spend some time observing the flames in our fireplace.

NEXT SPREAD:

The background words form the opening of the Mass. To me they suggest the appropriate attitude with which we as sinners come to God.

When I was fifteen, my girlfriend (who later became my wife) invited me to her one-room country church. What an impression it made on me to kneel for prayer in front of wood benches on a bare wood floor. I felt part of a group of believers who were wholeheartedly submitting themselves to God.

This spiritual also makes an allusion to early morning worship, something I thoroughly recommend to you.

Search me O God
and know my heart today
Try me O Saviour
know my thoughts, I pray
See if there be
some wicked way in me
Cleanse me from every sin
and set me free

KYRIE
ELEISON

Let us break bread together
on our knees
Let us drink the cup together
on our knees
When I fall on my knees
with my face to the rising sun
O Lord have mercy on me

MERCY

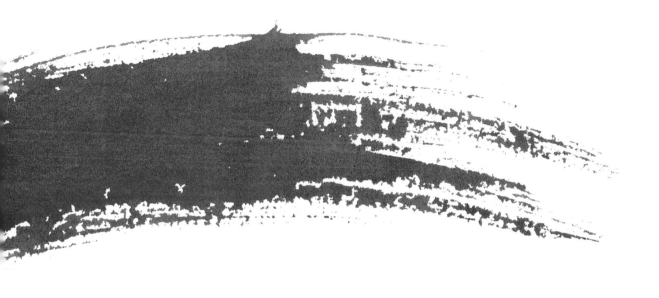

just as i am
  without one plea
but that thy blood
      was shed for me
and that thou biddest me
    come to thee
O LAMB OF GOD
       . i come
    i come

PREVIOUS SPREAD:

The use of Latin in this last part of the Mass preserves the mystery of Christ's sacrifice. On the other hand, the English words help us to understand what we need to know.

Two things are recalled here—the sacrifice of the Passover lamb and freedom. The early Jews spread the blood on the doorposts of their homes and were freed from Egyptian slavery.

In 1834, after her conversion, or liberation from spiritual bondage, Charlotte Elliott, an invalid, wrote the words on the right. Since 1952 millions more have responded to the message of this same song at Billy Graham crusades.

THIS SPREAD:

The words of this hymn are attributed to the twelfth-century mystic Bernard of Clairvaux. Since that time, they have been translated from Latin to German to English. Five centuries later Bach added the music from a folksong in his <u>Passion Chorale.</u>

Something else has been borrowed—the design of this piece. Ten years ago I was asked to design a thank you note for a missionary organization that operates in these nine different languages of Europe.

To me, <u>thank you</u> is one of the most beautful words found in any language.

GRAZIE

WHAT LANGUAGE SHALL I BORROW

EPHARISTO

TO THANK THEE DEAREST FRIEND

Merci beaucoup

FOR THIS THY DYING SORROW

Alstublieft

THY PITY WITHOUT END?

Tack så mycket

O MAKE ME THINE FOREVER

Danke Schön

AND SHOULD I FAINTING BE

Muchas gracias

LORD LET ME NEVER NEVER

OBRIGADO

OUTLIVE MY LOVE TO THEE

Thank you

Bill Gaither, a prolific contemporary writer of Christian music, wrote this song. Its testimony is that Jesus heals people today even as he did on earth two-thousand years ago. The joy inherent in the words bears out the principle that those who have been forgiven much love much.

The overlap of brush strokes in the first phrase accentuates both their handmade quality and humanness. The imagery of flooding suggested to me the curve of ocean waves breaking against the shore.

SHACKLED
BY A
HEAVY
BURDEN
'NEATH
A LOAD OF
GUILT
AND
SHAME

THEN THE
HAND OF JESUS
TOUCHED ME
AND NOW I AM
NO LONGER
THE SAME

HE TOUCHED ME
O HE TOUCHED ME
AND OH THE JOY
THAT FLOODS MY SOUL
SOMETHING HAPPENED
AND NOW I KNOW
HE TOUCHED ME
AND MADE ME
WHOLE

John Newton, an eighteenth-
century seaman and slave trader,
scoffed at Christianity. Then he
almost died at sea and promised
God that if his life were spared,
he would become a slave to the
gospel. Eventually he became a
preacher and wrote these
autobiographical words.

The American folk melody
brought to my mind guitar
strings and western neckerchief
motifs.

Both John Newton and Charles Wesley, the writer of this hymn, use the word <u>amazing</u> to describe an encounter with God. Thus I used a brush style similar to the previous page.

The powerful language here expresses God's movement toward us. At the end of this hymn, the unanswered question haunts us for a response. The words affected me so strongly that the design virtually spilled out onto the page.

NEXT SPREAD:
In 1845 Irishman Joseph Scriven moved to Canada. After the death of his fiancée, he devoted his life to helping the poor. He wrote this hymn for his ailing mother in far-off Dublin, describing his method of songwriting this way—"The Lord and I did it between us."

Critics complain about the poetry, but it was good enough for Henry Ford, who liked to play the song on his Jew's harp.

Writing down some of my own "sins and griefs" proved a perfect way to get me to start praying about them.

LONG
my imprisoned spirit lay
fast bound in sin and nature's night

THINE EYE
DIFFUSED A
QUICKENING
RAY

I woke
the dungeon
flamed with light

MY CHAINS
FELL OFF

my heart was free

I ROSE · WENT FORTH · AND FOLLOWED THEE

Amazing
Love

HOW CAN IT BE
THAT THOU
MY GOD
SHOULDST DIE
FOR ME?

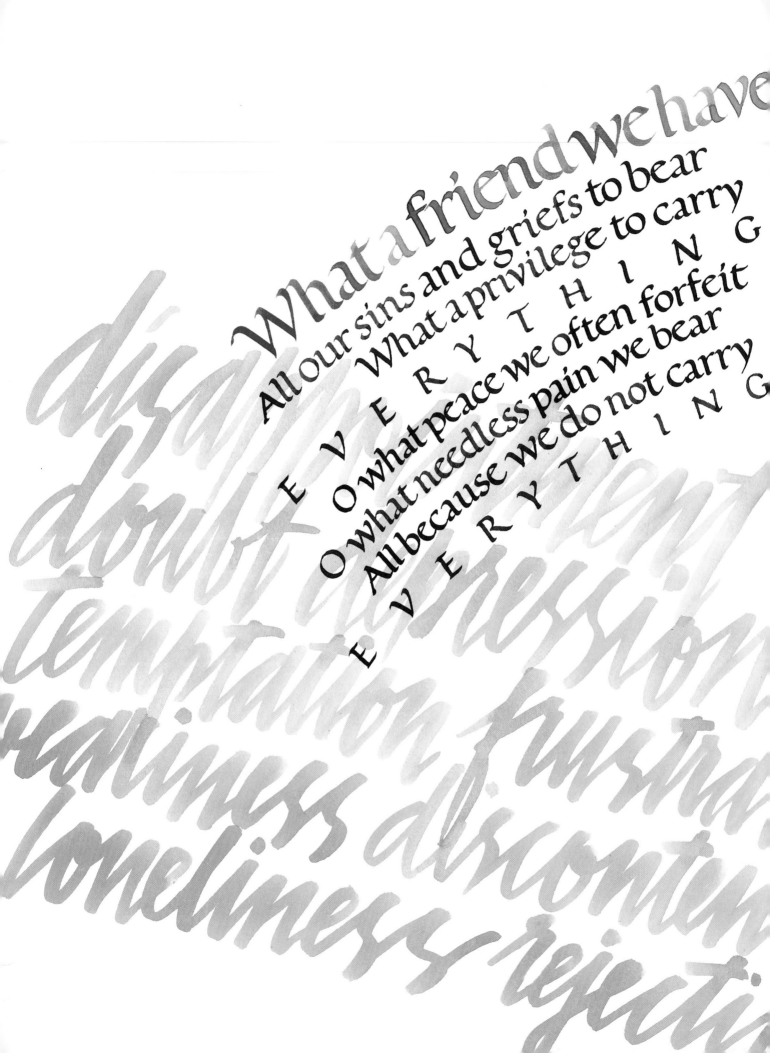

What a friend we have

All our sins and griefs to bear

What a privilege to carry

EVERYTHING

O what peace we often forfeit

O what needless pain we bear

All because we do not carry

EVERYTHING

EVERYTHING

in Jesus

to God in prayer

to God in prayer

Horatio G. Spafford lost four children at sea when two ships collided in 1874. Two years later he wrote these words to his children's memory.

This amazing statement can only be the result of grace, a gift of God. I am a Christian not because of how good I am, but because of Christ's acceptance of me. That is why the final words are written in gold.

When peace like a river attendeth my way

WHEN SORROWS
LIKE SEA BILLOWS ROLL

WHATEVER
MY LOT
THOU HAST
TAUGHT ME
TO SAY
IT IS WELL

IT IS
WELL
WITH
MY SOUL

God moves
in a
mysterious
His Wonders
He plants His footsteps in
And rides

God
His own

The poet William Cowper suffered from severe depression and attempted suicide several times. After recovery, his realization of God's providence led to these words. Elizabeth Barrett Browning was among those who paid tribute to his writing.

Here a single oriental brush gave me the broadest possible range of interpretation. The slightest change in pressure yielded a different stroke.

The brush marks in the background set the stage for my innermost feelings about the text. This is my response to God, who is independent and wholly other, yet interested in communicating with us.

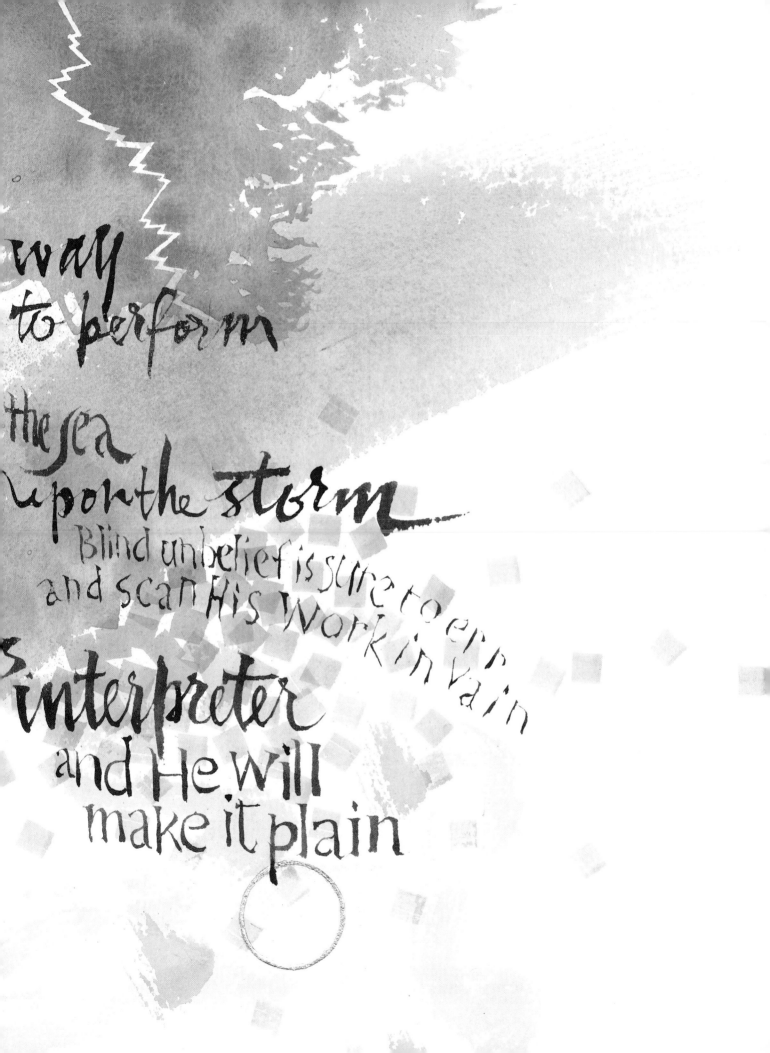

way
to perform

the sea
upon the storm

Blind unbelief is sure to err
and scan His work in vain

interpreter
and He will
make it plain

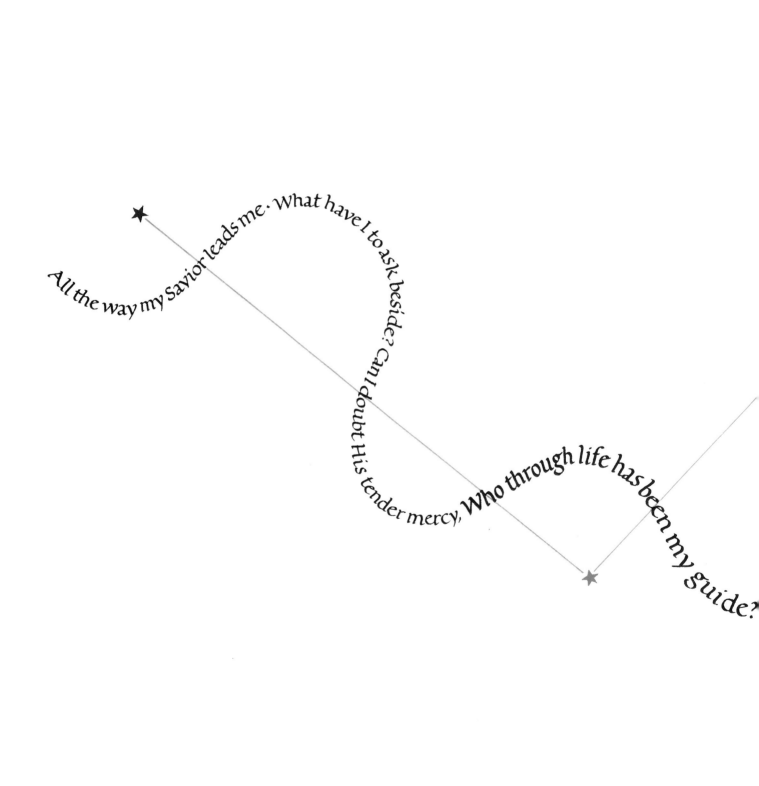

All the way my Savior leads me · What have I to ask beside? Can I doubt His tender mercy, Who through life has been my guide?

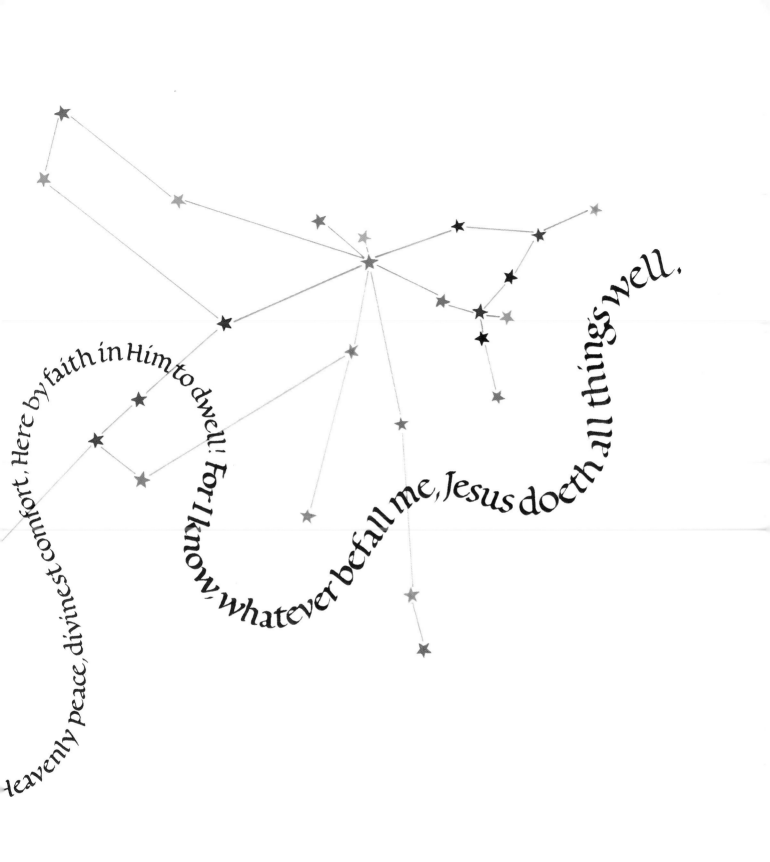

leavenly peace, divinest comfort, Here by faith in Him to dwell! For I know, whatever befall me, Jesus doeth all things well.

PREVIOUS SPREAD:
Fanny Crosby, who is probably America's best-known hymn writer, was born in 1823 and lived nearly all her life blind. Before her death in 1915, she had over eight thousand songs to her credit.

This piece is a map of my own forty years of traveling. As I plotted all the places I have ever been, I identified with this writer's recognition of the Divine Guide.

THIS SPREAD:
Frances Ridley Havergal wrote this hymn in the 1800s to affirm God's sovereignty.

One advantage I have over the musician is that my interpretation is not limited by the same melody for each stanza. I like to make my letterforms bounce as they do here on the first verse. That makes guidelines unnecessary, and the result appears livelier.

Like a river glorious
is God's perfect peace
Over all victorious
in its bright increase
Perfect, yet it floweth
fuller every day
Perfect, yet it
groweth deeper
all the way

EVERY JOY OR TRIAL FALLETH FROM ABOVE, TRACED UPON OUR DIAL BY THE SUN OF LOVE; WE MAY TRUST HIM FULLY ALL FOR US TO DO — THEY WHO TRUST HIM WHOLLY FIND HIM WHOLLY TRUE.

when upon life's billows

1 HOME

2 FAMILY

When you are discouraged

7 CHURCH

8 COMMUNITY

9 LOVE

Count your many

12 PURPOSE

13 CREATION

And it will surprise you

16 FATHER

17 SON

Johnson Oatman, Jr., wrote these words around the turn of the twentieth century. This song took on a new meaning for me when I met a family at a shelter for the homeless in a nearby town.

After telling me how they had just lost their house, they asked me to play this hymn. At one point during the singing, I saw the husband take his wife's hand. At that moment I realized true blessings are not material possessions.

By the way, can you add to my list of blessings?

4 EDUCATION

you are tempest tossed

3 WORK

5 THE ARTS

thinking all is lost

6 ABILITIES

blessings

10 FRIENDS

4 FORGIVENESS

15 LIFE

name them one by one

11 PEACE

What the Lord has done

18 HOLY SPIRIT

19 FREEDOM

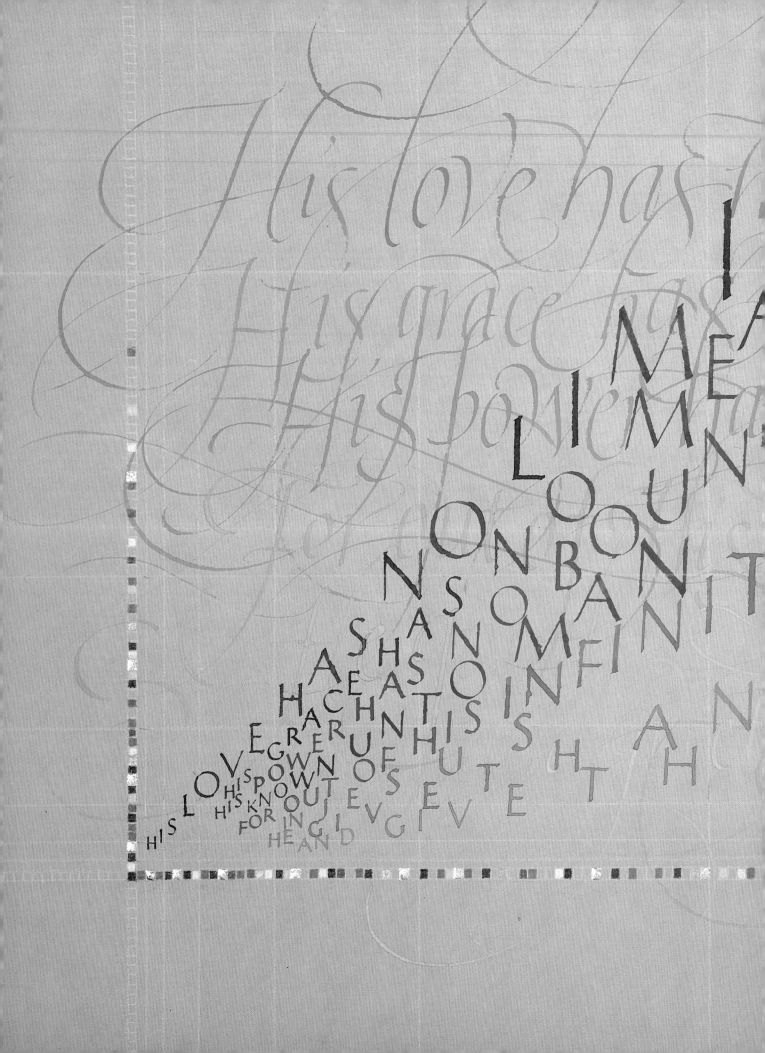

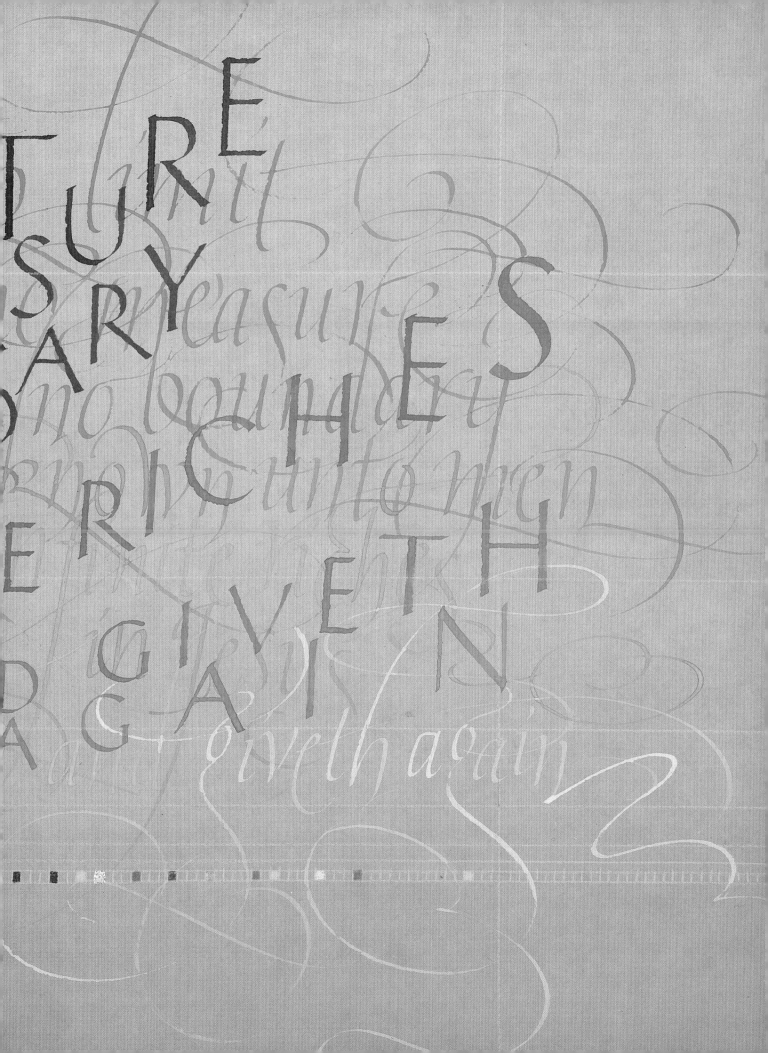

PREVIOUS SPREAD:

This song is one of the reasons I decided to let some of my work cover both pages and run off the edges of the paper. I knew of no other way to capture the overabundance conveyed in the lyrics.

Don't try to read the cursive writing. This is pure calligraphic play. I am glorying in God's exceeding generosity.

THIS SPREAD:

James Sammis, the writer of this hymn, was a businessman and YMCA worker who lived in the second half of the nineteenth century.

The marching quality of this tune inspired me to make Gothic letters appear to walk across the page. For me, this uncharacteristic use of the script visually combines both parts of the paradox: obedience and happiness.

when we walk with the Lord

in the light of His word

what a glory He sheds on our way

while we do His good will

He abides with us still

and with all who will trust and obey

Notice all the cookie-cutter people eating, working, running, and sleeping. Also see how the Master's servant stands out! Daniebelle Hall wrote both the words and the music in 1977.

When I want to write something without bringing attention to the calligraphy, I usually choose the bookhand style, which so closely resembles the words of the printed page.

just ordinary people
God uses
ordinary people
just like me
and you
who are
willing to do
as He commands
God uses people
that will
give Him all
no matter how small
your all may seem to you
because little
becomes much
as you place it in
THE MASTER'S HAND

MAY May the MAY the May the
THE MIND Word of God PEACE love
OF CHRIST dwell richly OF GOD fill
MY SAVIOR in my heart MY as
LIVE IN ME from hour FATHER
FROM DAY to hour, RULE
TO DAY, So that all MY LIFE IN
BY HIS LOVE may see EVERYTHING,
AND POWER I triumph THAT I
CONTROLLING only MAY BE
ALL I DO through CALM TO
AND SAY His power COMFORT
SICK AND
SORROWING

SO MAY I RUN THE RACE

of Jesus BEFORE ME

me STRONG AND

the BRAVE TO FACE

waters THE FOE —

fill the sea; LOOKING

Him exalting, ONLY UNTO

self abasing JESUS

This is AS I ONWARD GO

Victory

PREVIOUS SPREAD:

My response to the progression in these lyrics by Kate Wilkinson was to try to recreate that same movement across the spread here.

Day-to-day living is represented by simple capitals.

The strength of God's Word is demonstrated in gothic forms.

The peace of God is shown in full-bodied uncials.

The love of Jesus overflows in flourishing italic.

And finally, the race itself is illustrated with spaced rows of letters.

THIS SPREAD:

Braided hair, rugs, dough, and wreaths! They all probably influenced my thinking as I looked for a way to express the strength of a unified home.

Some may object to the puzzlelike arrangement. I was trying to slow down the reader long enough for him to get past the words to their meaning.

Henry Ware, Jr., who wrote these words, was a Massachusetts preacher during the first half of the nineteenth century.

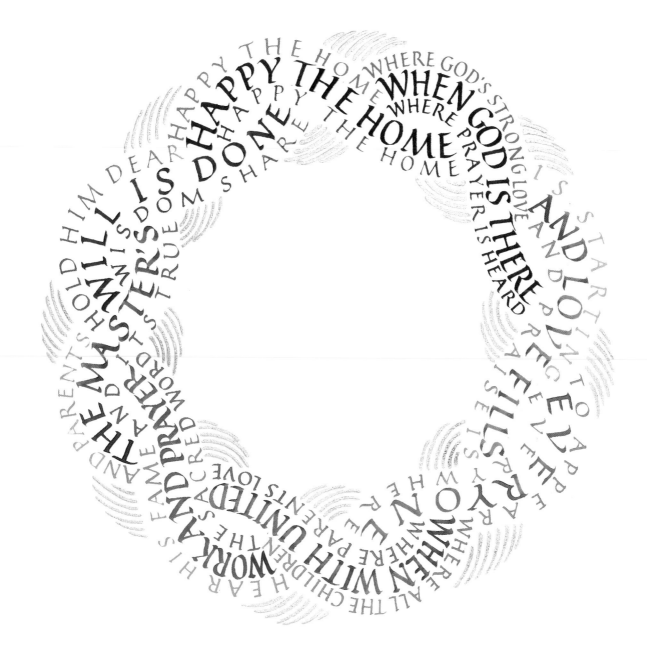

When I first heard Bob and Jane Farrell sing Tim Sheppard's love song to each other, I fell in love with it. Its message has two special elements: God's gift of love to us and our choice of commitment to each other.

I chose a more contemporary style of italic writing executed through pen manipulation, or twisting of the pen.

Nancy, this one is for you.

1920

1930

1940

1950

1960

1970

1980

1990

2000

2010

After all those years
When I look into your eyes
And see the one
I've chosen to adore
After all those years
When our children
have said good-bye
After all those years
I'll love you even more
After all those years

You, you are a gift of love
Sent from the Father
You, you are the stars above
I'll love you forever
We, we are no longer
two, but one
Walking hand in hand
Following the Son

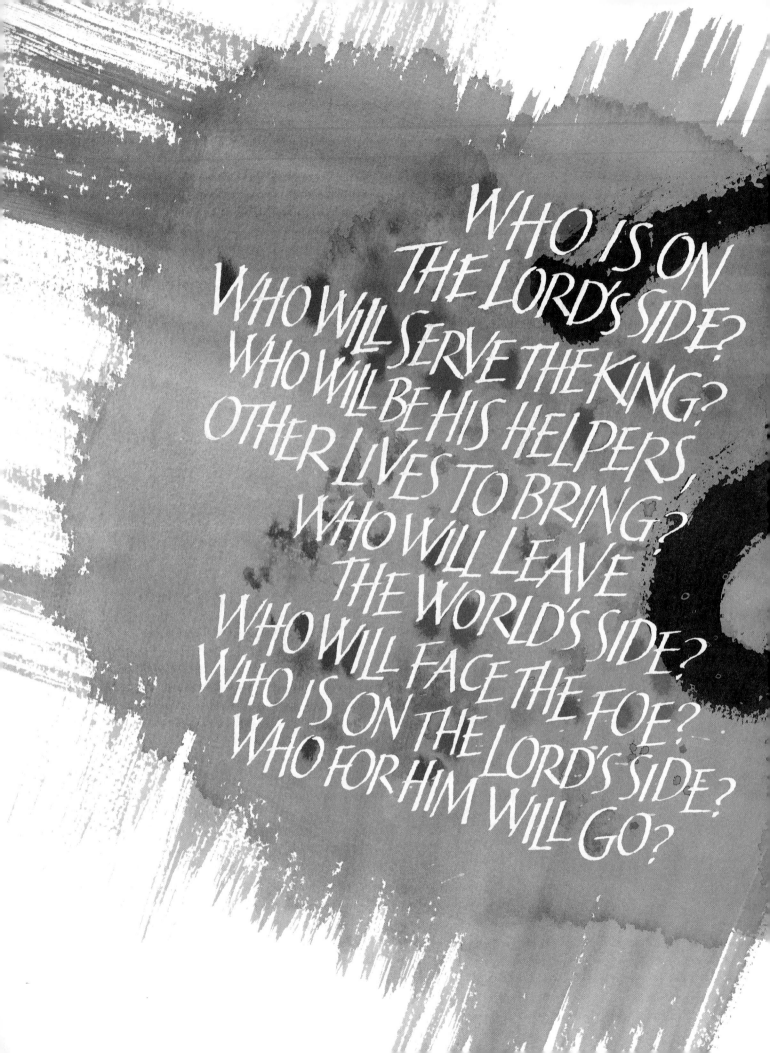

WHO IS ON
THE LORD'S SIDE?
WHO WILL SERVE THE KING?
WHO WILL BE HIS HELPERS,
OTHER LIVES TO BRING?
WHO WILL LEAVE
THE WORLD'S SIDE?
WHO WILL FACE THE FOE?
WHO IS ON THE LORD'S SIDE?
WHO FOR HIM WILL GO?

By Thy call
of mercy
By Thy grace
divine
We are on the
Lord's side
Savior,
we are Thine

PREVIOUS SPREAD:

Songs like this one by Frances Havergal have paraphrased Jesus' Great Commission and inspired many young people to be missionaries. Arnold Bank, my esteemed teacher of calligraphy, expressed puzzlement over my decision to teach English for a church mission in Japan for three years.

"Are you an artist or a missionary?" he asked.

"Both," I replied, since the gospel gives this calligrapher something important to say.

THIS SPREAD:

I remember singing this song by Adelaide Pollard during my early teens with others huddled around the campfire at church camp. The flames stand for more than the campfire, however. They are the Holy Spirit's powerful work in the life yielded to him.

Even though several people preferred a completed picture, the shape of my pot remains unfinished. I am still becoming what God has planned.

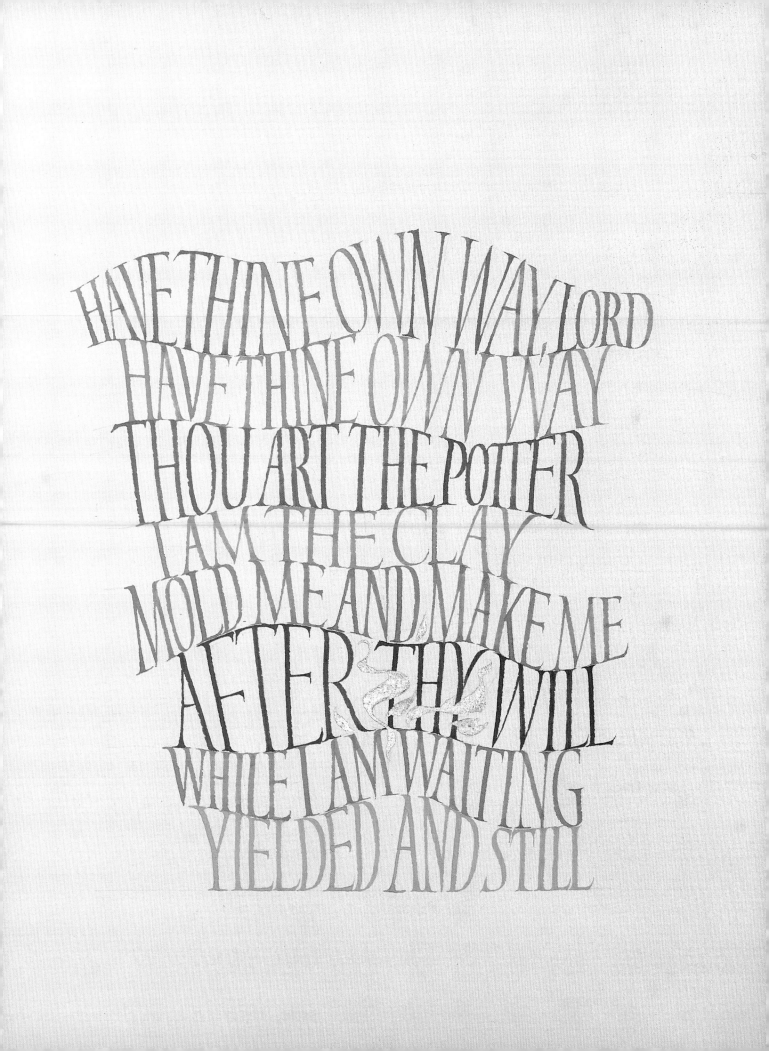

God used songs like this one to call me to devote my artistic talent to his glory. Frances Havergal discarded these words, thinking them poorly written, until her father found them one day. In response to the challenge of her own words, "Take my silver and my gold," she subsequently gave away nearly fifty articles of jewelry to a missionary society.

Some of these visual renditions of familiar hymns may seem jolting without the music. In this case, however, the melody's straightforward rhythm comes through for me.

Take my hands and let them move at the impulse of Thy love

Take my feet and let them be swift and beautiful for Thee

Take my voice and let me sing always, only, for my King

ABCDEFGHIJKLMNOPQRSTUVWXYZ

Take my lips and let them be filled with messages from Thee

Take my silver and my gold; not a mite would I withhold

Take my intellect and use every power as Thou shalt choose

Take my love; my Lord, I pour at Thy feet its treasure store

Take myself and I will be ever, only, all for Thee

I love Thee
I love Thee
I love Thee
my Lord
I love Thee
my Savior
I love Thee
my God
I love Thee
I love Thee
and that
Thou dost know
But how much
I love Thee
my actions
will show

PREVIOUS SPREAD:

The source of this hymn is unknown, but it appeared in Ingalls's Christian Harmony *in 1805.*

The first part of this verse is meant to look pretty and perhaps as superficial as the word love *has become in our culture. The last line, as illustrated here, is where the rubber meets the road.*

THIS SPREAD:

Steve Camp's grandmother was a hymn writer. Today he writes spiritual songs for a new generation. These lyrics remind me of Moses, Isaiah, and Paul, who were all stunned by the presence of the Lord.

Identifying with the songwriter's emotion, I painted the final background partly with my fingers. Then I added the writing entirely in black to aid legibility.

O LORD
YOUR WAYS
ARE NOT LIKE MINE
and it pounds like thunder
within my breast
all the anger of my humanness
and
though I call you LORD
I must confess
I'm a s t r a n g e r
to your
holiness

Can we really be
what we were
meant to be:
JESUS' PEOPLE
living by the S P I R I T
and living free
My heart longs to serve,
but w a n d e r s so aimlessly

O LORD
YOU DESERVE
EVERY PART OF ME
EVERY
EVERY
Hear my cry of desperation
as I see the wickedness of my ways

YOU ALONE
ARE MY SALVATION
and LORD
I've learned just one thing
to be true
that
THE CLOSER I GET TO YOU
I see
I'm a s t r a n g e r
to your
holiness

Fountains and the act of turning inspired the writing of the top verse attributed to Bernard of Clairvaux of the twelfth century. The universality of human experience comes through here. Nineteenth-century glitz was just as unsatisfying then as our vanities are today.

The second hymn below was written by Robert Robinson at age twenty-three. He became a believer through the preaching of George Whitefield. Our much-valued freedom to live as we please is responsible for the tug of war I tried to convey between allegiance to God and our stubbornness.

Thou joy of loving hearts
Thou fount of life Thou light of men
the best bliss that earth imparts
We turn unfilled to Thee again

O to grace how great a debtor
Daily I'm constrained to be
Let Thy goodness, like a fetter
Bind my wandering heart to Thee

Prone to wander
Lord, I feel it
Prone to leave the God
Here's my heart
O take and seal it
Seal it for Thy courts above   I love

O Breath of Life
REVIVE THY CHURCH

O Breath of Life

come, cleanse,

and

FIT THY

Revive us, Lord!
Is zeal abating?
while harvest

Revive

THE WORLD

This hymn by Bessie Porter Head, who lived from 1850 to 1936, acknowledges the recurring need for the Church to be rejuvenated by the Holy Spirit.

Can you sense the rush of power I experienced putting down some of these marks? Do you see the beauty of single-minded people acting out their love in our world?

come sweeping through us
WITH LIFE AND POWER
renew us
CHURCH TO MEET THIS HOUR
fields are vast and white
is Lord WAITING
EQUIP THY CHURCH
TO SPREAD
THE LIGHT
THE LIGHT
THE LIGHT T
THE LIGHT
THE LIGHT T
LIGH
IGH
H
T

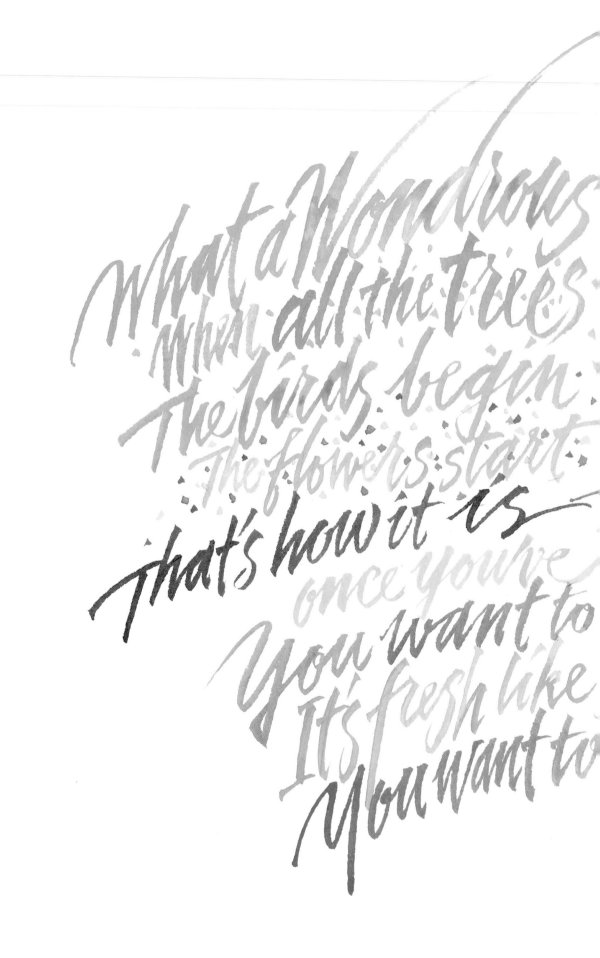

time is shining
are budding
to sing
their blooming
with God's love
experienced it
sing
spring
pass it on

Our God is gracious,
He bridged the hopeless gulf
He gave His Son

PREVIOUS SPREAD:
A handmade moose-hair brush gave me just the right balance between control and flexibility for this piece. The color changes from line to line are an attempt to help the reader pick out each line. In order to sustain both the spontaneity and the legibility, I had to give full concentration to the moment.

This second verse of "Pass It On" by Kurt Kaiser presents one of the best metaphors for Christian conversion—the season of spring. The excitement of this new life I pass on to you.

THIS SPREAD:
Margaret Clarkson is one of this century's finest hymn writers. This verse and its refrain move from historical retelling to a worshipful response. To parallel this transition, I used controlled lettering for the verse, then wildly interpretive writing for the chorus.

The found objects push the excitement even farther. The postage stamps seemed appropriate since they came from missionary letters I have received during the past fifteen years.

infinite in mercy;
our sin had made;
to purchase our salvation—
In Jesus Christ we meet God UNAFRAID
DECLARE
HIS GLORY
AMONG THE NATIONS
THROUGH ALL CREATION
His triumph sing

till all earth's peoples
all earth's peoples
all earth's peoples
bow in adoration
AND
JESUS CHRIST
BE
Everlasting King

The church's one foundation
she is His new creation
From heaven He came and sought
With His own blood He bought

YET SHE ON EARTH
AND MYSTIC SWEET
O HAPPY ONES

is Jesus christ her Lord,
by water and the Word;
her to be His holy bride;
her, and for her life He died.

HATH UNION WITH GOD THE THREE IN ONE
COMMUNION WITH THOSE WHOSE REST IS WON
AND HOLY! LORD GIVE US GRACE THAT WE,
LIKE THEM, THE MEEK AND LOWLY,
ON HIGH MAY DWELL WITH THEE.

PREVIOUS SPREAD:

Samuel Stone wrote this deeply moving hymn during a period of religious controversy. The words affirm the historic Apostles' Creed and the Church's universality. When first sung in London during 1888, it is recorded that people felt weak at the knees from its power.

Growing up in the church, I was never particularly struck by this hymn. Later, I found myself singing it with Japanese brothers and sisters in their language. Since then I have felt a strong bond to them—and to the hymn.

THIS SPREAD:

Peter Scholtes's words became a theme song during the Jesus People movement of the 1960s.

Using the simple form of the circle, I joined together many of the "flavors" of Christians—all those who acknowledge Jesus Christ as their Savior and Lord. By eliminating word spaces, I deliberately played down their particular identities to emphasize the whole.

If you get caught up with who is in the circle, you are missing the point of the song.

We are
one in the Spirit
We are
one in the Lord
and we pray
that all unity
may one day
be restored

adventists anglicans armenians baptists brethren charismatics congregationalists episcopalians evangelicals independents lutherans mennonites methodists nazarenes orthodox pentecostals presbyterians reformed roman catholics salvationists

and they'll know
we are christians
by our love

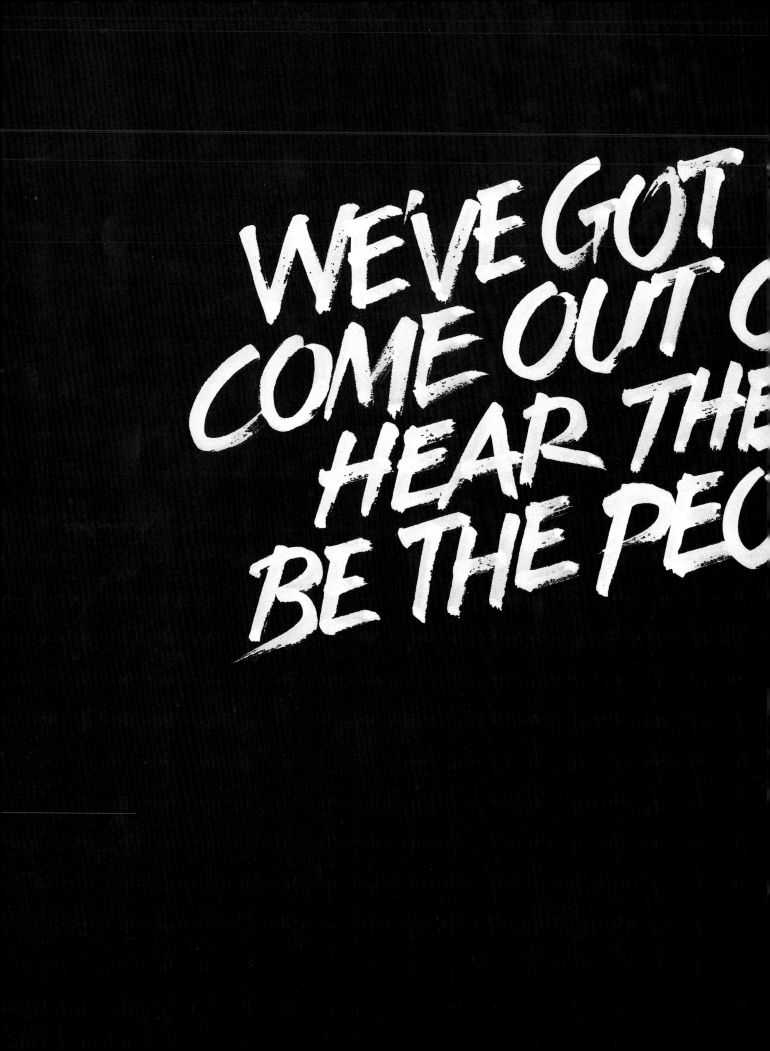

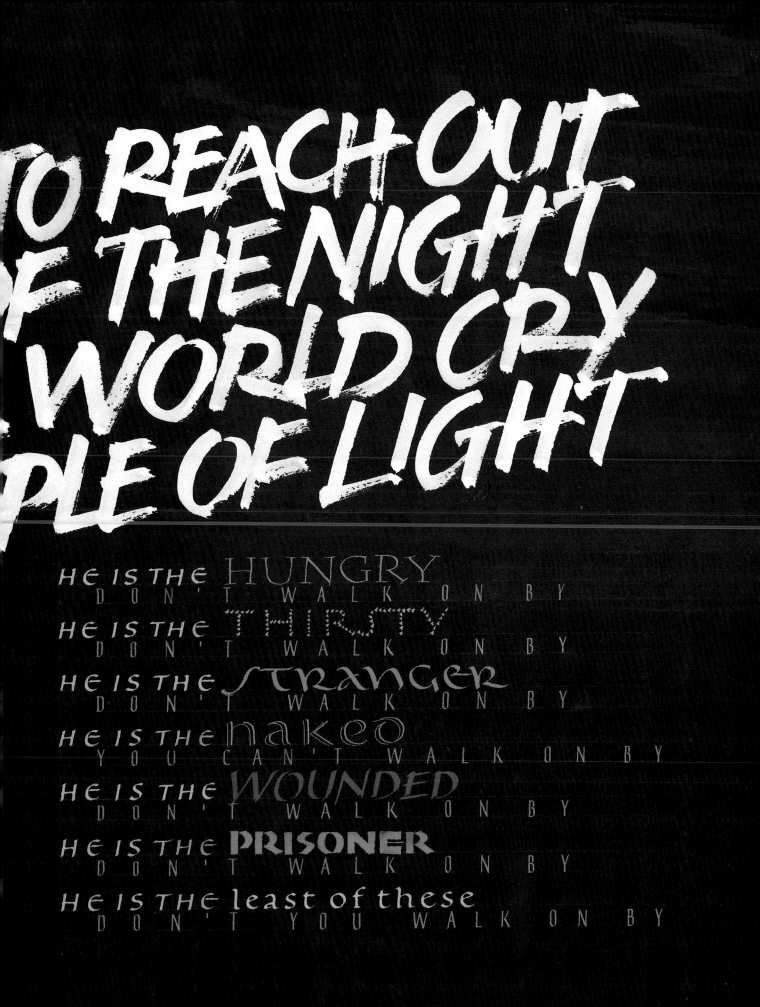

PREVIOUS SPREAD:
Contemporary songwriters Glenn and Wendy Kaiser have lived and worked among the social rejects of Chicago for two decades.

I chose the graffiti style of writing on the diagonal as a backdrop for the riveting repetition of the lyrics that follow.

THIS SPREAD:
Martin Luther took the hymn from the choir and gave it to the people. He wrote this hymn during great persecution and depression in 1529, basing it on Psalm 46 that affirms, "God is our refuge and strength." The large white Gothic letters were a natural choice for the lead line because of their German origin and the strength they convey. I am especially pleased with the use of letters on top of letters as a fresh way to embellish.

A mighty

Did we in our own strength confide

fortress

Our striving would be losing

is our God

Were not the right man on our side

A bulwark

The man of God's own choosing.

never

Dost ask who that may be?

failing

CHRIST JESUS, it is He.

This very personal prayer written
by John Bode around 1869
illustrates how close one can feel
toward Jesus. Hands and feet are
recurring themes in my work
because I like their universal
ability to represent our
humanness.

I am continually amazed that
the King of heaven chose to
become our servant. He washed
his friends' feet as an example.

No wonder we are compelled to
do the same.

O JESUS
Thou hast
promised to all
who follow Thee,
That where
Thou art in glory,
There shall
Thy servant be;
And, Jesus,
I have promised
To serve Thee
to the end;
O give me grace
to follow,
My Master and
my Friend.

Thou art coming O my Savior
We shall see Thee, we shall
We shall show Thee all
What an anthem
Singing out
Pouring out our
At Thine own

When the trumpet
of the Lord shall sound
and time shall be no more
And the morning breaks,
eternal, bright and fair
When the saved of earth
shall gather over
on the other shore
And the roll is called
up yonder
I'll be there.

God's own time is
the very best of times,
In him, living, moving,
we exist as long as he wills.
In him shall we die—
at the right time when he wills.
Ah, Lord teach us to remember
that our death is certain
that we might gain wisdom.
Set ready thine house
for thou shalt perish
and not continue living.
This is the ancient law:
Man, thou must perish.
Yes, come Lord Jesus.
Into thine hands now
do I commit my soul,
for thou hast redeemed me.
Lord, thou my faithful God,
This day shalt thou
with me in paradise be.
In peace and joy do I depart,
As God doth will it
Consoled am I in heart
and mind, calm and quiet
As God me
his promise gave:
My death is changed
to slumber.

0
33
2
4 35 36
37 38 39
40 41 42
43 44 45
46 47 48
49 50 51
52 53 54
55 56 57
58 59 60
61 62 63
64
65 66
67
68
69
70

PREVIOUS SPREAD:
What a contrast between the previous gospel song and this funeral cantata by Bach! My exposure to this classic piece came as the result of a commission to make a banner using these words.

I chose to write out the proverbial three score and ten years of a person's life in Arabic numerals. Writing them to parallel the disintegration of passing years was quite sobering.

THIS SPREAD:
I wanted the crowns to be recognizable but unlike any earthly ones. They bring to mind many of my past doodles. For this to come out was refreshing because I am usually more rational in my approach to design.

The significance of Jesus' resurrection comes across here— He "lives that death may die." Hallelujah!

Crown Him
the Lord of Life
Who triumphed
over the grave
Who rose victorious
to the strife
For those
He came to save
His glories
now we sing
Who died and
rose on high
Who died
eternal life to bring
And lives
that death may die